Living by God's Plan

by
Chris Rooke

PublishAmerica
Baltimore

© 2009 by Chris Rooke.
All rights reserved. No part of this book may be reproduced, stored in a retrieval system or transmitted in any form or by any means without the prior written permission of the publishers, except by a reviewer who may quote brief passages in a review to be printed in a newspaper, magazine or journal.

First printing

ISBN: 1-60703-975-3
PUBLISHED BY PUBLISHAMERICA, LLLP
www.publishamerica.com
Baltimore

Printed in the United States of America

About the Author

I was born and raised in south Texas in a broken home. I cannot remember ever living with my father. My mother raised my sister, my brother, and myself with the help of my grandmother and uncle. They saw to it that we were regularly involved in church activities from the day we were born to the day we were grown. We studied the Bible all of our lives.

I accepted Jesus Christ as my savior at the age of nine years. I took these teachings very seriously all of my life. When in high school, I felt that God wanted me to answer the call to preach the gospel.

Our family did not have much wealth in worldly goods, but we were rich in blessings which we received from God. Upon graduating from high school, I basically had two choices. I could have stayed on a dried-up farm at a time when there was no water with which to irrigate, or I could leave home and get a job. My choice was to leave home and get a job. I found myself in the recruiting station in San Antonio which was about twenty-five miles from home. I spent the next four years in the Air Force.

After basic training, I shipped out to Keesler Air Force Base in Biloxi, Mississippi, where I spent the rest of my four years. I found a good church home in Biloxi and continued to study the Bible and grow spiritually. When my four-year enlistment was up, I enrolled at Mississippi College in Clinton, Mississippi, where I earned a BA degree with a major in history and a minor in Bible.

Upon completion of college, I married my wife whom I met while in college. We moved to New Orleans, Louisiana, where I attended the New Orleans Baptist Theological Seminary for one year, after which I felt led to teach school, which I did for three years. It was at that time that I was led to Texas Instruments in Dallas, Texas, where I was employed for six years. I was fortunate enough while at Texas Instruments to be introduced to the computer industry as a computer programmer. I stayed with this profession until retirement thirty-five years later.

We left Texas and moved back to Mississippi where we worked with computers in the banking business until retirement.

I understood, at the age of nine, that a requirement for being born again as a born-again Christian was being willing to accept on faith Jesus Christ as my savior and a willingness to commit my life to Christ. There was a lot that I did not understand, but I committed myself to Christ by faith and tried to pattern my life as I was led by God. Never since that commitment have I doubted the word of God. We are told in the Bible that some things we might not understand, but they will be revealed to us when God is ready to make that revelation. During my years of study and searching for

God's will, some of these mysteries have been revealed to me. Others are still mysteries and will be so until God sees fit to reveal them to me.

After years of studying the Bible coupled with years of studying history I am more certain than ever that God is the one and only God, and God did without doubt create this world.

I have been led by God to write a book which deals with how God sees his people and the way they are living. Is God pleased or displeased with how we are using his creation? Please read this book with an open and prayerful mind.

Living by
God's Plan

Chapter 1
Bible Study Tips

In order to understand the Bible there are some important subjects that we must keep in our minds. We must understand what the Bible is and where it comes from. For several centuries, men of God have recorded in various manners the information that is contained in the Bible. Some were written down, and some were preserved through the centuries by word of mouth. Some parts recorded actual events that occurred through the centuries, and some parts recorded man's revelations and experiences with God. There was much recorded that is not a part of the Bible. We must understand that the Bible is not and never was intended to be a complete history book. The Bible is a record of God's relationship to man and starts with the creation. It is a record that includes that part of history that relates to God's plan and God's relationship with man.

The Bible contains a record of how God's perfect creation

without sin yielded to the temptations of Satan, and it tells us what the results of man's sin were. It shows how Godly prophets tried to lead man back to God.

During the Old Testament period it was necessary for man to offer burnt offerings and unblemished sacrifices in order to be forgiven of their sins. The Bible records how God chose Godly men to lead his people. God's plan was at work throughout the Old Testament in preparation for the time when God would send his own son to be born to a virgin. God's son, Jesus Christ, was born perfect without sin and lived without sin so he could be a worthy sacrifice for the sins of man.

The New Testament begins with Jesus Christ, the son of God, who gave his life on the cross. He shed His blood as a sacrifice so man would no longer have to offer burnt offerings and sacrifices. The New Testament is full of records of men of God who taught those who would learn about the forgiveness of their sins through faith and commitment to God through Jesus Christ. It also records the fate of those who choose not to accept Jesus Christ as their Savior.

Basically, there are two ways that man uses to study the Bible. Some will study the Bible with the purpose in mind to prove that their preconceived opinion is correct. This way is very dangerous and usually does no good. Others will study the Bible with an open mind, asking God to lead them and help them to understand. With this attitude we will find that the Bible is easier to understand than we imagined.

The most productive way by far to study the Bible is to prepare ourselves by prayer and faith in God and his Word. There may be some parts that you find hard to understand. God tells us that some things are a mystery to us, but God will reveal it to us when He is ready.

The King James translation of the Bible was developed during the sixteenth century. Since then, several more modern versions have been developed. Some of the modern versions are better than others. The decision of which we choose to use depends entirely on personal preference. Personally, we prefer the King James translation and find it to be clear enough that we can understand most of it. We are told in the Bible that there are some mysteries that we will not understand until God reveals it to us. All Bible references in this book are taken from the King James translation.

Chapter 2
Who Is God?

A prerequisite to understanding the Bible is an understanding of what the Bible is and where it came from. The Bible is not primarily a history book although it includes a great deal of history that occurred during the time covered by the Bible. The Bible begins with the creation of the earth and man. We do not know exactly what God and Heaven were like prior to the beginning of the Bible. However, there are some clues throughout the Bible. We do know that God has always been. God had no beginning. God can be described in three ways: omnipresent (present everywhere), omnipotent (all powerful), and omniscient (all knowing).

Heaven is a place God has prepared for all of his faithful to live with Him forever after their earthly death. Words are not adequate to describe Heaven. God speaks to us about Heaven throughout the Bible. It is likely that some of the references to Heaven contain symbolic descriptions in order for man with his finite mind to understand what kind of a place it is. Heaven is described as a perfect place where streets are paved with gold, and it is full of mansions where the faithful who accept God and His son, Jesus Christ, will live for eternity. There will be no suffering, no sorrow, no sickness, and no pain. Heaven has been described by using words and phrases that describe a perfectly glorious place. That is what awaits those who accept God's gift of salvation through acceptance of Jesus Christ as their Savior and Lord.

The Bible begins with the book of Genesis, chapter 1, verse 1. Genesis 1:1

1 In the beginning God created he heaven and the earth.

In Genesis 1:1, the phrase "in the beginning" refers to the beginning of the earth and man. It does not refer to the beginning of God who has no beginning and no end. God has always been. God is referred to as the alpha and omega, the beginning and the end.

God presents Himself to us in three different personalities: God the Father who lives in Heaven, God the Son who came to the earth as Jesus to be a sacrifice for our sins, and God the Holy Spirit who moves in our hearts convicting us of our sins and showing us the need for salvation through Jesus Christ. The Father, Son, and Holy Spirit are referred to as the trinity and they are all three a part of God.

God is perfect, and God created man to be perfect. God chose to create man with the freedom to choose right or wrong. Man was created with the freedom to choose man's way, or God's way. Each choice that man makes carries with it an appropriate result. Man will be held accountable for his choices.

Genesis 17:1-6 relates God speaking to Abram who was to become one of the greatest men of God in ages to come.

Genesis 17:1-6

1 And when Abram was ninety years old and nine, the Lord appeared to Abram, and said unto him, I am the Almighty God; walk before me, and be thou perfect.

2 And I will make my covenant between me and thee, and will multiply thee exceedingly.

3 And Abram fell on his face: and God talked with him, saying,

4 As for me, behold, my covenant is with thee, and thou shalt be a father of many nations.

5 Neither shall thy name any more be called Abram, but thy name shall be Abraham; for a father of many nations have I made thee.

6 And I will make thee exceedingly fruitful, and I will make nations of thee, and kings shall come out of thee.

God knew that Abram was a godly man who would seek God's will and follow God's leadership. God chose Abram to be the father of the branch from which Jesus Christ would be born.

God first told Abram what he expected from Abram. God expected Abram to be godly and make decisions based on God's will. God made a covenant with Abram and changed his name to Abraham. Because God is all-knowing, he knew he could count on Abram to make decisions based on the will of God.

God then told Abram what God would do for Abram in return for his obedience to the will of God.

After God delivered the children of Israel from bondage in Egypt, God gave them some commandments which emphasized what God expected from them. These commandments came to be known as the Ten Commandments. The first commandments were related to how God's people were to live in relation to God. The other commandments related to how man was to live in relation to other men.

These commandments begin in Exodus 20:1-6.

Exodus 20:1-6

1 And God spake all these words, saying,

2 I am the Lord thy God, which have brought thee out of the land of Egypt, out of the house of bondage.

3 Thou shalt have no other gods before me.

4 Thou shalt not make unto thee any graven image, or any likeness of any thing that is in heaven above, or that is in the earth beneath, or that is in the water under the earth:

5 Thou shalt not bow down thyself to them, nor serve them: for I the Lord thy God am a jealous God, visiting the iniquity of thy fathers upon the children unto the third and fourth generation of them that hate me;

6 And showing mercy unto thousands of them that love me, and keep my commandments.

The children of Israel had begun to worship idols and graven images. God commanded them to not worship these idols. God reminded them that He is a jealous God and would not tolerate His people splitting their allegiance between God and manmade idols.

In Exodus 20:22 God reminded Moses that God lived in Heaven from where He spoke to Moses and the children of Israel.

Exodus 20:22

22 And the Lord said unto Moses, Thus thou shalt say unto the children of Israel, Ye have seen that I have talked with you from heaven.

The book of Psalm contains many references to the nature of God and His relation to man.

Psalm 19:1

1 The heavens declare the glory of God; and the firmament showeth his handiwork.

Psalm 46:1

1 God is our refuge and strength, a very present help in trouble.

God is our refuge and can give us strength to overcome any problem if we will call on Him.

Psalm 86:9-10

9 All nations whom thou hast made shall come and worship before thee, O Lord; and shall glorify thy name.

10 For thou are great, and doest wondrous things: thou art God alone.

Psalm 86 is believed to be a prayer offered by David. Verses 9 and 10 refer to the majesty of God who is the one and only God.

Psalm 103:11 speaks of the magnitude of God's mercy for those who respect him.

Psalm 103:11

11 For as the heaven is high above the earth, so great is his mercy toward them that fear him.

Psalm 111:10 also speaks of those who respect God as the

beginning of wisdom. Those who keep His commandments have a good understanding.

Psalm 111:10

10 The fear of the Lord is the beginning of wisdom: a good understanding have all they that do his commandments: his praise endureth forever.

Proverbs 30:5-6 clearly tells us more about the nature of God and how we are to interpret the Bible.

Proverbs 30:5-6

5 Every word of God is pure; he is a shield unto them that put their trust in him.

6 Add thou not unto his words, lest he reprove thee, and thou be found a liar.

The Bible does not leave any question about the meaning of these words. They are very clearly stated. Every word of God is pure. God will shield those who put their trust in Him. If we add anything to these words, God will find us to be a liar and will not be pleased.

Jeremiah 23:23-24 tells us more about God in these verses relating what God said to Jeremiah.

Jeremiah 23:23-24

23 Am I a God at hand, saith the Lord, and not a God afar off?

24 Can any hide himself in secret places that I shall not see him? saith the Lord. Do not I fill heaven and earth? saith the Lord.

God made it clear to Jeremiah that God is always close by. God is everywhere in Heaven and on the earth. We cannot hide from God. He knows every act we commit and every thought we have.

Matthew 5:12 shows us more about the power of God and how he rewards those who faithfully serve him.

Matthew 5:12

12 Rejoice, and be exceeding glad: for great is your reward in heaven: for so persecuted they the prophets which were before you.

In Mathew 5:12, following what we call the Beatitudes, Jesus speaks to us concerning our rewards in Heaven after the persecutions endured while on earth. These rewards are for those who faithfully serve God even when we are persecuted for doing so. God reminds us that the prophets were also persecuted before us.

The sixth chapter of Matthew records the model prayer which Jesus used to teach the apostles the proper way to pray. This prayer begins with the acknowledgment that God is in Heaven.

Matthew 6:9

9 After this manner therefore pray ye: Our Father which art in heaven, Hallowed be thy name.

After Jesus finished teaching the model prayer to the apostles, he continued teaching the apostles how to forgive others.

Matthew 6:14

14 For if ye forgive men their trespasses, your heavenly Father will also forgive you.

When we pray to God for forgiveness of our sins, we must be in the spirit of forgiveness. We must first forgive those who have sinned against us. If we do not forgive others, then God will not forgive us. Prayer is a very personal thing between us and God. We must search our own heart first and then God will hear our prayer.

Jesus goes on to instruct his apostles concerning what they are to preach.

Matthew 10:7

7 And as ye go, preach, saying, The kingdom of heaven is at hand.

The kingdom of Heaven is at hand. Many Bible scholars would like to tell us exactly what the kingdom of Heaven is like. We will not know until we get there and see Heaven. We only know that Heaven is the most beautiful place in the world, and its majesty exceeds anything we have ever witnessed or ever will witness here on the earth. We know that someday Heaven will be our home if we are children of God. We will have no more sadness, no more tears, and no more persecution.

Jesus teaches the apostles by leaving no doubt as to his identity as Jesus Christ the son of the living God.

Matthew 16:15-17

15 He saith unto them, But whom say ye that I am?

16 And Simon Peter answered and said, Thou art the Christ, the Son of the living God.

17 And Jesus answered and said unto him, Blessed art thou, Simon Barjona: for flesh and blood hath not revealed it unto thee, but my Father which is in heaven.

Notice that Jesus told the apostles that flesh and blood did not reveal to them who He was. It was the Father who is in Heaven who revealed it to them. Man can tell others about Jesus Christ, but God through the work of the Holy Spirit must come into our heart before we accept Jesus Christ as our Savior. The Holy Spirit will respond to us as we confess our sins through prayer asking God to forgive us and save us from our sins.

The Pharisees came to Jesus and tried to tempt Him to say something that would cause problems with the law of the land.

Matthew 22:36-40

36 Master, which is the great commandment in the law?

37 Jesus said unto him, Thou shalt love the Lord thy God with all thy heart, and with all thy soul, and with all thy mind.

38 This is the first and great commandment.

39 And the second is like unto it, Thou shalt love thy neighbor as thyself.

40 On these two commandments hang all the law and the prophets.

The Pharisees wanted Jesus to say that one of the Ten Commandments was the greatest commandment in the law. Jesus would not be tricked. Jesus summarized the Ten Commandments by saying we must love the Lord our God with all of our heart, soul, and mind. Jesus continued by saying this is the first and great commandment, and the second commandment is like it. We must love our neighbor as we love ourselves. Jesus continued by saying that all of the law hangs on these two commandments.

At the crucifixion of Jesus those who witnessed the event were convinced that Jesus was truly the Son of God.

Matthew 27:54

54 Now when the centurion, and they that were with him, watching Jesus, saw the earthquake, and those things that were done, they feared greatly, saying, Truly this was the Son of God.

The centurion and the people who were with him watched Jesus as the life flowed from his body. When Jesus died the sky turned dark and there was an earthquake. When these things occurred the centurion and those with him became afraid and said that truly this was the Son of God.

The book of Mark in the New Testament gives Mark's account of the gospel of Jesus Christ. Mark begins in the first verse by acknowledging that Jesus Christ is the Son of God.

Mark 1:1

1 The beginning of the gospel of Jesus Christ, the Son of God.

Mark 13:31 tells us that the words of Jesus will never pass away.

Mark 13:31

31 Heaven and earth shall pass away: but my words shall not pass away.

The words of Jesus are the words of God.

The book of John begins by speaking about the Word. This reference to the Word is a reference to God. John begins by giving an introduction to God.

John 1:1-5

1 In the beginning was the Word, and the Word was with God, and the Word was God.

2 The same was in the beginning with God.

3 All things were made by him; and without him was not any thing made that was made.

4 In him was life; and the life was the light of men.

5 And the light shineth in darkness; and the darkness comprehended it not.

Simply stated, John tells us that God always was, and God made everything. Because of sin man lives in darkness unless he lets the light shine in. God is the light. God sent His Son to us as the light of the world for those who will let the light shine in. Those who will not let the light shine in will continue to live in darkness.

John 3:16 is one of the most loved Bible verses because it gives man hope in spite of the sinful nature into which man is born.

John 3:16-17

16 For God so loved the world, that he gave his only begotten Son, that whosoever believeth in him should not perish, but have everlasting life.

17 For God sent not sent not his Son into the world to condemn the world; but that the world through him might be saved.

God loves the world so much that He sent His only Son, born to a virgin, raised among man, and nailed to a cross. Jesus arose from the dead after three days, met with some of His faithful followers, and then ascended back into Heaven to be with His Father where Jesus would hear our prayers.

John 4:24 describes God as a Spirit.

John 4:24

24 God is a Spirit: and they that worship him must worship him in spirit and in truth.

Since God is a Spirit, when we worship Him we must worship Him as a spirit. This means our hearts must be tuned in with God before our worship will be accepted. We do not need any manmade images in order to worship God. Our worship must be heart to heart between us and God.

In his letter to the churches in Galatia, Paul told them how God would deal with those who live in sin.

Galatians 6:7-9

7 Be not deceived; God is not mocked: for whatsoever a man soweth, that shall he also reap.

8 For he that soweth to his flesh shall of the flesh reap corruption; but he that soweth to the Spirit shall of the Spirit reap life everlasting.

9 And let us not be weary in well-doing: for in due season we shall reap, if we faint not.

God knows every sin that we commit. We cannot fool God. If we choose a life of sin away from God, we will reap an eternity in hell with Satan away from God. If we choose a life in the will of God, we will reap life everlasting in Heaven with God.

Paul, in his letter to the churches in Ephesus, explains that there is only one way to become a child of God.

Ephesians 4:4-7

4 There is one body, and one Spirit, even as ye are called in one hope of your calling;

5 One Lord, one faith, one baptism,

6 One God and Father of all, who is above all, and through all, and in you all.

7 But unto every one of us is given grace according to the measure of the gift of Christ.

Do not be fooled by the false belief that it does not matter so much how you live your life so long as you attend church. Paul explains that there is one body, one Spirit, one Lord, one faith, one baptism, and one God and Father of all. God created man with the freedom to accept Him on His terms, or reject Him. Man does not have the power of choice to change God's plan for the redemption of man. Man only has the choice to either accept Christ, or, to reject Christ.

The book of Revelations is perhaps the most difficult part of the Bible for most of us to understand. Revelations 21:6-7 plainly refers to power of God and the rewards He has in store for those who follow him.

Revelations 21:6-7

6 And he said unto me, It is done. I am the Alpha and Omega, the beginning and the end. I will give unto him that is athirst of the fountain of the water of life freely.

7 He that overcometh shall inherit all things; and I will be his God, and he shall be my son.

God is the alpha and omega, the beginning and the end. He will give the water of life freely to those who put their trust in God, and they will live forever in Heaven. God will be their God and they will be His son.

A lot of Bible references have been included in this chapter in order to explain clearly who God is, where He is, and the nature of God when dealing with mankind. There are many other references in the Bible concerning the nature of God. We have chosen these references, but you will find numerous others while reading the Bible

Chapter 3
Who Is Satan?

Who is Satan? Where did he come from? Bible scholars have offered varied opinions for the answer to this question. Who Satan is and where he came from are not as important to our understanding the Bible as his effect on our lives and our allegiance to God. Some Bible scholars believe Satan was once an angel named Lucifer who was expelled from Heaven by God. It is true that Lucifer was an angel in Heaven who believed that he was more powerful than God. His ambition was to become as powerful as God. The result of Lucifer's ambition was to be expelled by God from Heaven into the pit of Hell where he would spend eternity.

Based on the evidence that God reveals to us in the Bible, it is possible that Lucifer became Satan's leading angel in Hell. It really has no bearing on our salvation and our relationship with God. What is important to us is the nature of Satan and how he affects our lives through temptations.

Isaiah 14 gives the account of how Lucifer fell from Heaven and how God expelled him to the pit of Hell for eternity.

Isaiah 14:12-15

12 How art thou fallen from heaven, O Lucifer, son of the morning! How art thou cut down to the ground, which didst weaken the nations!

13 For thou hast said in thine heart, I will ascend into heaven, I will exalt my throne above the stars of God: I will sit also upon the mount of the congregation, in the sides of the north:

14 I will ascend above the heights of the clouds; I will be like the most High.

15 Yet thou shalt be brought down to hell, to the sides of the pit.

The book of Job reveals some of the nature and presence of Satan.

Job 1:6-7

6 Now there was a day when the sons of God came to present themselves before the Lord, and Satan was among them.

7 And the Lord said unto Satan, whence comest thou? Then Satan answered the Lord and said, From going to and fro in the earth, and from walking up and down in it.

When Satan answered God he indicated that he had been all over the earth. There is nowhere we can go on earth where Satan cannot tempt us. We can resist these temptations only by asking God to give us the strength to resist.

Matthew 4:1-11 records the temptations of Jesus by Satan. Jesus lived a perfect life without sin. In order to be a worthy sacrifice for our sins it was necessary that Jesus had no sin. It was necessary that he be unblemished in order to be a sacrifice for our sins.

Matthew 4:1-11

1 Then was Jesus led up of the Spirit into the wilderness to be tempted of the devil.

2 And when he had fasted forty days and forty nights, he was afterward an hungered,

3 And when the tempter came to him, he said, If thou be the Son of God, command that these stones be made bread.

4 But he answered and said, It is written, Man shall not live by bread alone, but by every word that proceedeth out of the mouth of God.

5 Then the devil taketh him up unto the holy city, and setteth him on a pinnacle of the temple,

6 And saith unto him, If thou be the Son of God, cast thyself down: for it is written, He shall give his angels charge concerning thee: and in their hands they shall bear thee up, lest at any time thou dash thy foot against a stone.

7 Jesus said unto him, It is written again, Thou shalt not tempt the Lord thy God.

8 Again, the devil taketh him up into an exceeding high mountain, and showeth him all the kingdoms of the world, and the glory of them;

9 And saith unto him, All these things will I give thee, if thou wilt fall down and worship me.

10 Then saith Jesus unto him, Get thee hence, Satan: for it is written, Thou shalt worship the Lord thy God, and him only shalt thou serve.

11 Then the devil leaveth him, and, behold, angels came and ministered unto him.

Jesus had been in the wilderness for forty days during which He fasted in preparation for His earthly ministry. When He emerged from the wilderness, He was hungry. Satan tempted Him to turn some stones into bread so He could eat them. Jesus answered Satan by saying that man shall not live by bread alone, but by every word uttered by God. Satan then took Jesus to the roof of the temple and tempted Him to jump knowing that He would not be harmed. Jesus told Satan that he must not tempt the Lord God. Satan then took Jesus up on a high mountain and showed Him all of the kingdoms of the world and told Him that he would give them to Jesus if Jesus would only fall down and worship him. Jesus told Satan to get away from Him because God commands us to worship God and only God shall we worship. The devil then left Jesus.

It was necessary for Jesus to be tempted and to resist these temptations if He was to be a fit sacrifice for the sins of man. By successfully resisting the temptations of Satan, Jesus became a fit sacrifice like a lamb without a blemish.

After the temptations of Jesus He began to teach his disciples what was to happen to Him on the cross.

Matthew 16:21-23

21 From that time forth began Jesus to show unto his disciples, how that he must go unto Jerusalem, and suffer many things of the elders and chief priests and scribes, and be killed, and be raised again the third day.

22 Then Peter took him, and began to rebuke him saying, be it far from thee Lord. This shall not be unto thee.

23 But he turned, and said unto Peter, Get thee behind me, Satan: thou art an offense unto me: for thou savorest not the things that be of God, but those that be of man.

Jesus knew that He came to earth to live a perfect life without sin and then be crucified to become a sacrifice for the sins of those who would accept Him. When Jesus explained to His disciples what He must do Satan tempted Peter to protect Jesus and not allow Him to go to Jerusalem. Jesus again told Satan to leave Him alone. Jesus then reminded Peter that he should seek those things that are of God and not those things that are of the world.

Luke 22:3-5

3 Then entered Satan into Judas surnamed Iscariot, being of the number of the twelve.

4 And he went his way, and communed with the high priests and captains, how he might betray him unto them.

5 And they were glad, and covenanted to give him money.

Satan tempted Judas to identify Jesus for the officials so they could arrest him. Judas gave in to the temptation and identified Jesus for the high priests and the captains after which they paid him a monetary reward for betraying Jesus.

In Paul's second letter to the Christians at Corinth he speaks about forgiveness and why we should have a spirit of forgiveness.

2 Corinthians 2:9-11

9 For to this end also did I write, that I might know the proof of you, whether ye be obedient in all things.

10 To whom ye forgive any thing, I forgive also: for if I forgave any thing, to whom I forgave it, for your sakes forgave I it in the person of Christ;

11 Lest Satan should get an advantage of us: for we are not ignorant of his devices.

Jesus taught us to forgive others. Satan tempts us to hold a grudge and refuse to forgive. If we refuse to forgive then we are giving in to the temptations of Satan. God expects us to be strong and stand against the temptations of Satan.

In Paul's first letter to the church of the Thessalonians he explains how he would like to be with them in person but Satan prevented him from being there.

I Thessalonians 2:18

18 Wherefore we would have come unto you, even I Paul, once and again, but Satan hindered us.

We do not know how Satan prevented Paul from making the journey. We only know that Satan put a stumbling block in Paul's way.

If Satan can continuously place temptations in our way, where can we get the power to resist these temptations?

Ephesians 6:10-18

10 Finally, my brethren, be strong in the Lord, and in the power of his might.

11 Put on the whole armor of God, that ye may be able to stand against the wiles of the devil.

12 For we wrestle not against flesh and blood, but against principalities, against powers, against the rulers of the darkness of this world, against spiritual wickedness in high places.

13 Wherefore take unto you the whole armor of God, that ye may be able to withstand in the evil day, and having done all, to stand.

14 Stand therefore, having your loins girt about with truth, and having on the breastplate of righteousness;

15 And your feet shod with the preparation of the gospel of peace;

16 Above all, taking the shield of faith, wherewith ye shall be able to quench all the fiery darts of the wicked.

17 And take the helmet of salvation, and the sword of the Spirit, which is the word of God.

18 Praying always with all prayer and supplication in the Spirit, and watching thereunto with all perseverance and supplication in the Spirit, and watching thereunto with all perseverance and supplication for all saints;

The whole armor of God refers to our obedience to God and our diligence in our personal relationship with God. We cannot be part-time Christians if we want to wear the whole armor of God. It requires faith, prayer, and studying God's Word. When we wear the whole armor of God, we will always be in a spirit of prayer. We can talk to God anytime. When we wear the armor of God we can overcome the temptations of Satan.

In Paul's letter to Timothy, Paul teaches Timothy how to stay out of the clutches of Satan.

2 Timothy 2:20-26

20 But in a great house there are not only vessels of gold and of silver, but also of wood and earth; and some to honor, and some to dishonor.

21 If a man therefore purge himself from these, he shall be a vessel unto honor, sanctified, and meet for the master's use, and prepared unto every good work.

22 Flee also youthful lusts: but follow righteousness, faith, charity, peace, with them that call on the Lord out of a pure heart.

23 But foolish and unlearned questions avoid, knowing that they do gender strifes.

24 And the servant of the Lord must not strive; but be gentle unto all men, apt to teach, patient.

25 In meekness instructing those that oppose themselves; if God peradventure will give them repentance to the acknowledging of the truth;

26 And that they may recover themselves out of the snare of the devil, who are taken captive by him at his will.

We are tempted by Satan to dishonor God, but God gives us the strength and power to withstand these temptations by saying no to Satan. This strength will only be as strong as our personal relationship to God. If we obey God and trust God, then there is nothing Satan can do to keep us in his power.

The Bible, in the second chapter of James, speaks to us concerning those who believe there is a God but this belief is not evident in their works.

James 2:17-20

17 Even so faith, if it hath not works, is dead, being alone.

18 Yea, a man may say, Thou hast faith, and I have works: show me thy faith without thy works, and I will show thee my faith by my works.

19 Thou believest that there is one God, thou doest well: the devils also believe, and tremble.

20 But wilt thou know, O vain man, that faith without works is dead?

God tells us that faith without works is dead. It is good to believe there is one God. Even the devils believe there is one God. If we truly have faith in God, we must show that faith by our works.

The Bible speaks to us in the book of James about the lustful nature of man which the devil uses to tempt man to sin. God also tells us how to make the devil flee from us and leave us alone.

James 4:3-7

3 Ye ask, and receive not, because ye ask amiss, that ye may consume it upon your lusts.

4 Ye adulterers and adulteresses, know ye not that the friendship of the world is enmity with God? Whosoever therefore will be a friend of the world is the enemy of God.

5 Do ye think that the scripture saith in vain, the spirit that dwelleth in us lusteth to envy?

6 But he giveth more grace. Wherefore he saith, God resisteth the proud, but giveth grace unto the humble.

7 Submit yourselves therefore to God. Resist the devil, and he will flee from you.

The world in this context refers to worldly pleasures and practices that are contrary to the will of God. Man has a lustful nature which is fueled by temptations from the devil causing man to commit sinful adulterous acts. Man is either a friend of the world or a friend of God. If a man is a friend of the world, he will yield to the temptations of the devil. If man is a friend of God, he will receive power from God to stand against the temptations of the devil. The devil knows the power of God and will flee from us when we put our faith in God.

In the book of Revelations God reveals to us the destiny of Satan at the end of time.

Revelations 12:9-10

9 And the great dragon was cast out, that old serpent, called the Devil, and Satan, which deceiveth the whole world: he was cast out into the earth, and his angels were cast out with him,

10 And I heard a loud voice saying in heaven, Now is come salvation, and strength, and the kingdom of our God, and the power of his Christ: for the accuser of our brethren is cast down, which accused them before our God day and night.

God describes Satan as one who deceived the whole world. In symbolic terms Gods tells us about the final defeat of Satan during the last days.

Chapter 4
How We Are Tempted

Temptations of man began in the Garden of Eden. God created Adam and Eve in His own image which means they were without sin when God placed them in the Garden. God could have created man without the freedom to make choices, but God chose to give man the freedom to make choices. God showed Adam and Eve all of the trees in the Garden and told them they could eat the fruit from any tree except the tree of knowledge of good and evil.

Until then Adam and Eve were perfect and had no knowledge of good and evil. Satan appeared to Eve in the form of a serpent and tempted her to eat fruit from the tree from which God had forbidden them to eat. The following reference from Genesis relates the first time Satan tempted God's creation. It reminds us of how Satan slips up on us when we least expect him. We must always be on our guard against the temptations of Satan.

Genesis 3:1-10

1 Now the serpent was more subtle than any beast of the field which the Lord God had made. And he said unto the woman, Yea, hath God said, Ye shall not eat of every tree of the Garden?

2 And the woman said unto the serpent, We may eat of the fruit of the trees of the garden:

3 But of the fruit of the tree which is in the midst of the garden, God hath said, Ye shall not eat of it, neither shall ye touch it, lest ye die.

4 And the serpent said unto the woman, Ye shall not surely die:

5 For God doth know that in the day ye eat thereof, then your eyes shall be opened, and ye shall be as gods, knowing good and evil.

6 And when the woman saw that the tree was good for food, and that it was pleasant to the eyes, and a tree to be desired to make one wise, she took of the fruit thereof, and did eat, and gave also unto her husband with her; and he did eat.

7 And the eyes of them both were opened, and they knew that they were naked; and they sewed fig leaves together, and made themselves aprons.

8 And they heard the voice of the Lord God walking in the garden in the cool of the day: and Adam and his wife hid themselves from the presence of the Lord God amongst the trees of the Garden.

9 And the Lord God called unto Adam, and said unto him, Where art thou?

10 And he said, I heard thy voice in the garden, and I was afraid, because I was naked; and I hid myself.

There are many symbolic examples used by God in the Bible to illustrate what God wants us to understand. We do not know for sure whether Satan actually appeared to Eve as a serpent or if God uses the serpent as a symbolic representation of Satan. It really does not matter. Verse 1 describes the serpent as being the most subtle of any animal on the earth. This certainly gives us an accurate picture of Satan who is sneaky and deceiving in the way he slips up on us to tempt us. When Eve told the serpent that God had commanded them not to eat fruit from the tree and said that if they ate fruit from the tree they would surely die, Satan told Eve that they would not really die but instead their eyes would be opened and they would be like God knowing good and evil.

Eve ate the fruit from the forbidden tree and Satan then used Eve to tempt Adam by giving him some of the fruit. Adam also ate the fruit. Their eyes were opened, and they did know good and evil. It is important to note that from this time forward the nature of man changed. Man had been without sin. From this time forward man was sinful and it was necessary that man confess his sins to God and ask for forgiveness. The sinful nature of man was passed on to every person who was born after Adam and Eve. It really is not important whether or not a symbolic representation was used by God. The important thing to remember is the message that God communicated to us.

During the centuries before Jesus Christ, man made sacrifices to God as a means of gaining forgiveness. The New Testament relates how God gave man his Son, Jesus Christ, to live among men and be sacrificed on the cross as a sacrifice for the sins of man. After Jesus Christ had been born of a virgin, lived a perfect life without yielding to the temptations of Satan, died on the cross shedding His blood to be a sacrifice for the sins of all who would accept him, and arose from the dead on the third day after His burial, it was no longer necessary to offer sacrifices for the forgiveness of our sins.

If we are to be on guard against the temptations of Satan it is helpful to understand how sneaky Satan is and how he sneaks up on us. We once heard a story that shows how sneaky Satan is and how he is able to sneak up on us so easily. It goes something like this. Once upon a time Satan called a meeting of all of his most trusted angels. The agenda for the meeting was the fact that too many people were accepting Christ and learning to resist his temptations. Satan asked his angels to think the problem over and make suggestions how he could keep so many from accepting Christ as their Savior. Several of his angels made suggestions and Satan replied that he had tried that and it would not work. Finally one angel sitting in the back of the room raised his hand and was recognized by Satan. The angel told Satan that he should tell people that they were right to accept Christ, but there was no rush. Take your time and think about all you will have to give up. Just don't rush into it. Take your time. There is no reason to hurry. Satan smiled and expressed his approval of the suggestion. Satan said that he would use this suggestion and it would surely work.

That is only a story, but it surely shows how sneaky Satan is and how he is able to trap so many of us in sin. The Bible relates how God has destroyed civilizations that had sunken so far into sin that God chose to destroy them. There are countless areas of our lives that Satan is always at work tempting us.

Let's turn our attention to some of the areas of our lives where temptations by Satan are prevalent. We can expect temptations to be present anywhere there are God's people present.

We must not overlook the pulpits in our churches. The churches are led by our clergy who may go by different names in different churches. Those who are called by God to devote their lives to teaching and leading God's people in worship are looked up to by many as being immune to temptations. We tend to overlook the fact that all men are cursed with the sins that began with Adam and were passed down through all generations of mankind. Our church leaders must spend several hours in prayer and communication with God to give them strength to withstand the temptations of Satan. This is not because God judges their sins any differently from the way He judges the rest of us. It is because Satan finds more ways to tempt our church leaders. God calls godly men to preach his word and teach us how to put our trust in God. All too often we see a member of the clergy yield to the temptation to build their own empire in an effort to gain more personal wealth and fortune. We see members of the clergy who preach their own interpretation of the Bible in an effort to gain worldly fame. God calls men to preach the gospel of Jesus Christ who was crucified and arose from the tomb and ascended into Heaven to be with God as a sacrifice for the sins of those who put their trust in them. The gospel is very simple when presented in God's way. Satan tempts preachers to choose the most complicated verses in the Bible and preach their own interpretation as though it came from God. We sometimes get the notion that church leaders are perfect. God tells us in the Bible that there is none perfect, no, not one. None means not one. It is for this reason that churches must be careful and spend a lot of time in prayer before choosing someone to lead them.

Marriage is another institution which Satan likes to attack with his temptations. God created man and woman to populate the world. Man and woman were created to be joined together to form the basis for the first family in God's world. The New Testament clearly teaches that marriage is the first step towards creating a godly family. The Bible also teaches that a man should have one wife, and each wife should have one husband. Satan knows that if he can wreck a marriage then he will break up God's perfect union. If the husband and wife are godly they will want to obey the laws of God. In order to form a perfect union between husband and wife each party must be committed to the other. A godly marriage is the first step towards raising a godly family and enjoying a godly and happy home life. God tells us in the Bible to teach our children the godly way and they will not depart from it. Satan tempts us that we need not be in a hurry to start teaching our children because they will not start learning until they are older. Nothing could be farther from the truth. A child begins to learn the day he or she is born. In fact, children learn faster during the earlier years of their lives. They learn things during the first few years of life that they will remember all of their lives.

When we are at work we are away from our spouse and away from our children. Do not forget God is always with us if we have put our trust in Him. God is everywhere. A lot has been said about prayer and where we can and cannot pray. The fact is we can pray anywhere and any time we choose. God always is available for a source of strength in time of need. All we have to do is call upon Him. Some of the most effective prayers are not audible to anyone but God. You can utter a prayer from your heart without making any audible sound. That is why we must always be in the spirit of prayer which requires that our heart be right with God. While we are at work on the job we will probably be around many unbelievers. If we will always remain in the spirit of prayer, we can call upon God at any time from any place. If we find ourselves in a place where we cannot remain in the spirit of prayer, we need to get out of there and go somewhere else. When we are in the spirit of prayer Satan cannot succeed in his effort to get us to yield to temptation. We can look Satan in the eyes and ask God to give us strength to resist. Satan will always lose the battle if we use the whole armor of God.

Leisure time is probably the time when Satan finds it easier to tempt us. We should always be busy about God's work. There is an old saying that idle hands are the devil's workshop. There is always something we can do to keep busy. That does not mean we can never rest. Even while resting we can stay in tune with God. That is one of the most productive times to be in the spirit of prayer which simply means staying in touch with God. Not only do we talk to God, He also talks to us. That is why we must stay in tune with God.

Our schools are another place where Satan likes to tempt God's people. He has a lot of help from some of our politicians and judges. It would be easier for God's people to rid the schools of many temptations and problems if the federal politicians and federal judges would stay out of the school affairs and let the state governments run the schools like the United States Constitution dictates when it says that anything not explicitly covered by the Constitution shall be left up to each individual state. While it is proper for the judges to step in when the rights of the students are violated, they go too far when they rewrite the Constitution just because some small group of self-serving lawyers gets on their soapbox. We believe in the separation of church and state because it is taught in the Bible. However, it is stretching the point considerably to label displaying a copy of the Ten Commandments on the wall as a violation of separation of church and state. We cannot help but wonder which commandment the judges object to. The first four commandments refer to man's relation to God, but they do not pressure anyone to believe in God. That is an individual choice made by each one of us. The last six commandments deal with man's relation with one another. They deal with honoring your father and mother, not committing adultery, not stealing, not lying against your neighbor, and not coveting what belongs to your neighbor. It is no wonder that our children come out of school with little respect for anyone with authority. This attack on the Ten Commandments is not new to our generation.

When Jesus Christ was teaching His disciples the Pharisees came to Him and tried to trick Him into saying something which they could use to arrest Him. They asked Jesus which of the commandments is the greatest. Jesus summarized the commandments by saying the greatest is that you should love the Lord with all your heart all your soul and all your might and the second is like the first, you should love your neighbor as yourself. We would be better off if we posted a copy in every hallway of every school and taught the students that most of the basic laws in the Constitution were patterned after the last six commandments. Satan must be rejoicing after the success he has with these temptations.

Another great success scored by Satan in our schools involves the teaching of creation. The judges forced the schools to quit teaching the creation theory because it is recorded in the Bible. The same judges allowed the theory of evolution to be taught. God's people did not demand that the schools quit teaching the theory of evolution. They only asked that both theories be taught. The judges chose only to allow the atheist theory to be taught. This also made Satan rejoice.

Hollywood, news media, and television give Satan a wide-open field for a place to practice his temptations. They are all judged by their peers according to how much money they can make. They are full of sex and ungodly living because those are the characteristics that make money. There is nothing wrong with making money, but God tells us in the Bible that we should not put a stumbling block in front of our neighbor. We cannot even watch the commercials on television without seeing sex and sinful living.

Satan has been so successful with his temptations in our country that our courts have ruled that the Ten Commandments cannot be posted on the walls in our schools. This has always been a mysterious decision to me. When our forefathers wrote our Constitution, they patterned the basic laws of this great country after the Ten Commandments. They used specifically the fifth through the tenth commandments. Our judges have ruled that the Ten Commandments may not be displayed yet they permit condoms to be distributed and promiscuous sex to be encouraged.

Chapter 5
What God Sees in the Home

The very core of our life here on earth is the home. The very nature of our earthly life begins with influences which we experience in the home beginning with the first few moments of our life at birth. When a new baby is born it is God's plan at work.

God created man to have dominion over the earth. This was a part of God's plan, and it is still the same plan today as it was in the beginning.

Genesis 1:26-27

26 And God said, Let us make man in our image, after our likeness: and let them have dominion over the fish of the sea, and over the fowl of the air, and over the cattle, and over all the earth, and over every creeping thing that creepeth upon the earth.

27 So God created man in his own image, in the image of God created he him; male and female created he them.

In the first chapter of Genesis, verses 26 through 27, God tells us why He created man and woman. As we continue to read in the second chapter of Genesis, God gives us more information about the creation of man and woman.

Genesis 2:20-24

20 And Adam gave names to all cattle, and to the fowl of the air, and to every beast of the field; but for Adam there was not found a help meet for him.

21 And the Lord God caused a deep sleep to fall upon Adam, and he slept; and he took one of his ribs, and closed up the flesh instead thereof;

22 And the rib, which the Lord God had taken from man, made he a woman, and brought her unto the man.

23 And Adam said, This is now bone of my bones, and flesh of my flesh; she shall be called Woman, because she was taken out of Man.

24 Therefore shall a man leave his father and his mother, and shall cleave unto his wife: and they shall be one flesh.

God's blueprint for a family clearly begins with a husband and wife who are mutually devoted to each other to the extent that they can work in harmony. The fact that God first created man, and then created woman, does not mean that man is more important than woman. God created man and woman to be the cornerstone of the family. It takes both man and woman to form a family. God gave each some very special gifts that are needed to form a family.

Let us consider the family that is patterned after the teachings of God, which are found in the Bible. We will consider several Bible references. Please do not reach conclusions based on only one or two references. Consider all of the following references and then evaluate the family based on God's blueprint. Study of God's word will result in many more references that teach us God's plan for the family.

In Genesis 3:16 God speaks to the woman after the events that had happened in the Garden of Eden.

Genesis 3:16

16 Unto the woman he said, I will greatly multiply thy sorrow and thy conception; in sorrow thou shalt bring forth children; and thy desire shall be to thy husband, and he shall rule over thee.

We might consider this as the beginning of the first family. While God told Eve that her husband would rule over her, we must not place too much emphasis on the word "rule" until we examine all of the scriptures that God has given to us concerning the family.

In Proverbs 12:4 God emphasizes the importance of a virtuous woman and the lower importance of the less virtuous woman.

Proverbs 12:4

4 A virtuous woman is a crown to her husband: but she that maketh ashamed is as rottenness in his bones.

In I Corinthians 7:1-3 the Apostle Paul gives the church at Corinth some instructions from God for the purpose of correcting some problems which the church at Corinth was experiencing. In his letter, Paul told them that every man should have his own wife, and every woman should have her own husband. Each husband and wife must treat each other with mutual love and respect. It takes this mutual love and respect between husband and wife to have a godly family.

I Corinthians 7:1-3

1 Now concerning the things whereof ye wrote unto me: It is good for a man not to touch a woman.

2 Nevertheless, to avoid fornication, let every man have his own wife, and let every woman have her own husband.

3 Let the husband render unto the wife due benevolence: and likewise also the wife unto the husband.

In Ephesians 5:22-25 in a letter which the Apostle Paul wrote to the church at Ephesus, Paul tells them the husband is the head of the wife, even as Christ is the head of the church. He then told the wives to be subject to their own husband in everything. Paul then told the husbands to love their wives even as Christ loves the church.

Ephesians 5:22-25

22 Wives, submit yourselves unto your own husbands, as unto the Lord.

23 For the husband is the head of the wife, even as Christ is the head of the church: and he is the savior of the body.

24 Therefore as the church is subject to Christ, so let the wives be subject to their own husbands in every thing.

We would not begin to suggest that the husband is any more important than the wife. The husband is clearly instructed to love, protect, and honor the wife. When decisions are made in the family, the godly husband will consult the wife and consider every opinion which the wife has.

The husband and wife can always have varied opinions that need to be discussed and worked out to their mutual satisfaction before a decision is made. When both husband and wife have accepted Christ and put their faith and trust in Him, no disagreement is too big to reconcile with the leadership of God.

In God's plan, the husband and wife must function as one to form a godly family. The children must be loved and cared for, and they must be taught godly values. This is easier to accomplish when the husband shoulders his responsibility to work and support the family. That makes it easier for the wife to stay at home with the children and teach them the proper values as they grow older.

Our society tells us that it takes both husband and wife working in order to support the family. The values taught by our society are not always the same as the values taught by God. Our society tells us that we should have everything we want. When we listen to God, He tells us that we sometimes want more than we need. The lives of our children as they grow into adulthood are more precious than all of the worldly things that two incomes can buy. When we want too much and want to live a faster lifestyle, our lifestyle will indeed require both husband and wife to work.

The lifestyle and the habits of the husband and wife will be passed on to the children. One of the most important tasks for which the husband and wife are responsible is the proper teaching and training of the children. In Proverbs 22:6 God instructs us concerning the training of our children.

Proverbs 22:6

6 Train up a child in the way he should go: and when he is old, he will not depart from it.

Children begin the learning process the moment they are born. They begin learning from what they see and what they hear. It is part of God's plan that the teaching and training of the children are primarily the responsibility of the mother and father. This responsibility should not be taken lightly. It is often complicated and made more difficult by the peer pressure from those with whom our children associate. We must help our children become involved with friends who will build them up rather than take them down. Also, we must insure that the home reflects a godly atmosphere. The relationship of the mother and father to God will have a lasting effect on the children.

In Exodus 20:12, God speaks to the children concerning their responsibility to their parents.

Exodus 20:12

12 Honor thy father and thy mother: that thy days may be long upon the land which the Lord thy God giveth thee.

Children are to respect and obey their parents. This is one of the Ten Commandments. The children must be taught respect and obedience from birth to adulthood. We read in the book of Proverbs how God expects us to discipline our children.

Proverbs 13:24

24 He that spareth the rod hateth his son: but he that loveth him chasteneth him betimes.

God tells us that if we withhold discipline from our children, that is a sign that we hate our children. God continues by telling us if we love our children we will discipline them when appropriate.

There is much disagreement in our society about how we should discipline our children. We must remember that our society is not made up solely of godly people who have a personal relationship with God. It is important, first, that we set a godly example for our children to follow. When they fail to follow our godly example, then discipline should be applied. The method of discipline must be chosen based on the reason for discipline. God will discipline those parents who, themselves, fail to set a godly example.

There are some manmade factors in our society that present a great challenge when it comes to disciplining our children. There are manmade laws that sometimes seem to be contrary to God's laws. We must remember that many of our lawmakers are not godly men. Many of them do not accept God's law. When we encounter this problem, we must diligently talk to God concerning how we must proceed. God will also deal with the ungodly lawmakers as evidenced throughout the Bible.

Another manmade factor affecting discipline is evident in what is happening to our schools. Probably the most glaring action backed by the highest lawmakers in our country is evidenced by forbidding a copy of the Ten Commandments to be posted on the walls in our schools. It makes one wonder which commandment the lawmakers object to. At the same time, many of our schools have instituted practices that encourage premarital sex to the extent that some schools go so far as to furnish condoms to students.

The only effective way to combat this problem is for God's

people to act like God's people and vote for godly politicians when election time comes around.

Another manmade factor that presents a great challenge when trying to teach our children to be godly adults is evident when we turn on our television set. Television stations plan their programming based on how they can get a better rating when the stations are rated. What is godly and wholesome and conducive to showing a godly example for our children is seldom, if ever, considered.

Much like the news media, the movie industry has become one of the greatest work places for Satan to work his deception as he tempts our young people. This profession, including the movie stars, paints a picture of a world made up of parties, loose living, fun, and a place where everything is make-believe. The deception of Hollywood stardom is used by Satan to tempt many who expect to find a life of luxury, parties, and wealth. God has an answer to this sort of living. It is surprising how many adults yield to these temptations in an effort to move up the social ladder.

We must remind ourselves that God tells us that more people will choose the wide road to an everlasting torment in Hell, and fewer will choose the narrow gate that leads to life everlasting. The following is how Jesus taught it to his apostles.

Matthew 7:13-20

13 Enter ye in at the strait gate: for wide is the gate, and broad is the way, that leadeth to destruction, and many there be which go in thereat:

14 Because strait is the gate, and narrow is the way, which leadeth unto life, and few there be that find it.

15 Beware of false prophets, which come to you in sheep's clothing, but inwardly they are ravening wolves.

16 Ye shall know them by their fruits. Do men gather grapes of thorns, or figs of thistles?

17 Even so every good tree bringeth forth good fruit; but a corrupt tree bringeth forth evil fruit.

18 A good tree cannot bring forth evil fruit, neither can a corrupt tree bring forth good fruit.

19 Every tree that bringeth not forth good fruit is hewn down, and cast into the fire.

20 Wherefore by their fruits ye shall know them.

These words spoken by Jesus indicate that Hell is going to be mighty crowded, and Heaven is going to have plenty of space. He warns us that there will be many false prophets, and we must always be on our guard. We can recognize them by their deeds and not by what they say or what they seem to be. The false prophets will come in all kinds of disguises. Some may even be found in some of the pulpits in our churches. They will be exposed by God who will cast them into everlasting Hell.

It behooves each one of us to examine the fruit produced by our life and have a sincere talk with God. As children of God, we should continually be in a spirit of prayer. Much has been said by society about where and when we are allowed to pray. We can pray any time and anywhere we are as long as we are in the spirit of prayer. God's people should be praying unceasingly for our country. We must participate in every election and put some godly leaders in office on both the local and national level. God's people need to reclaim this country that was founded with God's blessings and under the leadership of God.

Chapter 6
What God Sees in Our Justice System

There must be laws to insure the protection and well-being of each individual in a community. The same rule applies whether the community is a city, state, country, or any other group of individuals. The laws should be fair and should render justice to each individual. God gives us a good example of justice in the words of Jesus as Jesus was teaching His disciples. This example is speaking of justice for those who break the commandments of God. There is no better example of justice for those who break man's law.

Matthew 5:19-22

19 Whosoever there shall break one of these least commandments, and shall teach men so, he shall be called the least in the kingdom of heaven: but whosoever shall do and teach them, the same shall be called great in the kingdom of heaven.

20 For I say unto you, That except your righteousness shall exceed the righteousness of the scribes and Pharisees, ye shall in no case enter into the kingdom of heaven.

21 Ye have heard that it was said by them of old time, Thou shalt not kill; and whosoever shall kill shall be in danger of the judgement:

22 But I say unto you, That whosoever is angry with his brother without a cause shall be in danger of the judgement: and whosoever shall say to his brother, Raca, shall be in danger of the council: but whosoever shall say, Thou fool, shall be in danger of hell fire.

No phrase better describes the Constitution and the related Amendments than "justice for all." The group of citizens which shoulders the responsibility of insuring that all citizens receive justice is the Supreme Court. This court is composed of a group of judges. Each member of the Supreme Court is nominated by the presiding President and confirmed by Congress. Once a judge becomes a member of this court, he or she remains a member until either they die or they resign. They are not held accountable for the decisions and rulings handed down by the court. They have the power to overrule the decisions of the lower courts. There is something wrong with that picture in this great land of ours which we call a democracy.

The rule allowing for the judges to serve for life, or until they choose to resign, has led to numerous cases of interpretation of parts of the Constitution that are different from that intended by our founding fathers when they formed the Constitution. This court has violated the rights of innocent victims by setting criminals free. It has violated the rights of many citizens by taking away from them that which they earned by hard work and giving to others under the guise of achieving equality. It seems a reasonable opinion that the members of the Supreme Court should, in some way, be held accountable for their decisions. A change to the terms of the Supreme Court judges should be considered in an effort to maintain integrity and wisdom in this court. This change would require an amendment to the Constitution. This will happen only if and when enough citizens insist that the candidates for Congress push for a change and then go to the polls and vote for those candidates who make it part of their platform.

The Supreme Court is empowered to enforce the Constitution. Their duties should not include interpreting the Constitution. Any part of the Constitution that is not clear enough for the meaning to be evident should be amended so the intention and meaning are clearly evident.

While on the subject of elections this is a good time to discuss the method we use in our presidential elections. This is possibly the most misunderstood part of the Constitution. Many citizens assume that the candidate receiving the most popular votes should be the winner of the election. This is not necessarily true. The winner of the election is finally determined by the electoral college. The simplest way to understand the electoral process is to think of each state as holding a separate election. Each state is allotted a number of votes determined by the same method by which the number of representatives is determined. The winning candidate in each state is given the number of votes allotted to the respective state. A few states are an exception to this rule. A state is allowed to split their vote, depending on the popular vote, if the state legislature so chooses. Only two or three states follow this exception to the rule. The purpose of using the electoral college is to insure that each state has a proportionate weight in the election based on the census of the state. This method, however, does have the possibility of having a winner who got the majority of the popular votes but did not get the majority of the electoral college votes. This permits each state to carry weight proportionate to the number of citizens in that state. We find no fault in this method of elections because it equalizes the weight that each state has in choosing our leaders.

According to Amendment X, the last right in the Bill of Rights, the powers not delegated to the United States by the Constitution, nor prohibited by it to the states, are reserved to the states respectively, or to the people. Simply worded, any legislation not expressly covered in the Constitution is left to the individual state to legislate. Part of Article VI, Clause 3 of the Constitution states that the senators and representatives before mentioned, and the members of the several state legislatures, and all executive and judicial officers, both of the United States and the several states, shall be bound by oath or affirmation, to support this Constitution. This simply means that all senators, representatives, state legislators, executive officers and judges are bound by the oath they took when assuming office to support the Constitution as it has been amended. This does not include the right of judges to loosely interpret the law that is clearly specified in the Constitution so that it satisfies their agenda.

The legislative branch of the United States has the power to make federal laws that apply to every state. The legislative branch of each state has the power to make state laws that apply only to their respective state. These laws must conform to the Constitution of the United States. If they do not conform to the Constitution they will be declared unconstitutional and will not become law. The Supreme Court has the power to declare laws unconstitutional if they do not conform. This is another reason why we believe the Supreme Court should be held accountable for their decisions.

Some of our legislators seem to believe their job depends on how many new laws they can sponsor and get passed through Congress. Use of tobacco is a good example. It is doubtful that anyone really believes that smoking is good for the respiratory system. It does not take a medical expert to understand that passing smoke through the system is harmful to the body. We see nothing wrong with creating smoke-free areas. Some good laws have been passed to regulate the use of tobacco. The problems arise when the supporters of a smoke-free society are never satisfied. Some group is always coming out with a new study which sometimes does more harm than good. Too much effort has been spent trying to convince the people that second-hand smoke is dangerous to our health. It is possible that we sometimes legislate too much. If smoking is dangerous to our health, it makes more sense to pass a law that prohibits the selling of tobacco products.

Over the past few decades some laws have been passed and enforced that seem to deny justice rather than guarantee justice.

Suppose you were fortunate enough to accumulate a considerable amount of wealth and you are traveling across the country when, for some reason, you are stopped by law enforcement agents who discover that you have in your possession a large amount of cash. Though we have not seen the law that permits such seizure, it can be assumed that such a large amount of cash is considered to be from illegal drug transactions or some other illegal act, and the cash can therefore be confiscated by the legal authorities. The cash will sometimes be returned to the owner after a considerable amount of legal manipulation which is costly as well as time-consuming. Cash is legal tender and we have a right to carry any amount that suits our purpose as long as it is not connected to any illegal activity. It may not be a wise practice to carry large amounts of cash, but we do have the right to do so if we so desire. In cases where drugs or other illegal activity are involved, confiscation may be legal, but where there is no crime involved, we have the legal right to carry cash.

Some of the laws that have been passed by Congress protect the criminal rather than the victim. While it is true that a person is innocent until they are proven guilty in a court of law, all evidence gathered that pertains to a case in court should be presented in order to insure that justice has been served. We have laws that do not allow certain evidence to be presented in court if it was gathered illegally. If we have real evidence that proves the person on trial committed the crime, then the evidence should be submitted in court. If it turns out that the evidence was found during an illegal search, the person responsible for the illegal search should be charged if they broke the law, but that should not be used as a technicality by which the guilty go free without paying for the crime. We should be more concerned with the rights of the victim.

Our prison system is another example of what has gone wrong with justice for all. A few decades ago, the inmates in our prisons worked at jobs that helped support the prison system. Inmates are in prison because they have been found guilty of committing crimes against society. Our prisons have become overcrowded, and prison riots have broken out too often. The Constitution allows for requiring inmates who have been found guilty of a crime to work while in prison. Several decades ago some prisons raised enough food to feed the prison population. Some of the inmates worked at other jobs that helped support the prison. When citizens knew they would be required to work while in prison they were not as anxious to be sent to prison. Under the current system, many of the inmates have it better in prison than on the outside. They have a roof over their head, plenty to eat, television, and many other activities which they may participate in. It is easy to see how too much idle time for the inmates can cause a riot. We would not have the overcrowded prisons if our prisons were more like prisons and less like country clubs.

Since the beginning of the twenty-first century our politicians have created a monster that has grown at an alarming rate and threatens our country like nothing we have seen in our lifetime. We are referring to the outsourcing of jobs to foreign countries all over the world. Unemployment in the United States has risen at an alarming rate because jobs have been shipped abroad. At the rate we are going we will reach the point of no return. We must get a handle on this problem before it is too late. The longer it is allowed to grow the harder it will be to regain control of our own fate. We believe it is time to place tariffs on all products imported from foreign countries. Our unemployment continues to rise, and our nation's deficit continues to rise. If this monster is allowed to continue to grow, we will see the day when we will no longer be a leader in high-tech industries. We should cease the practice of giving large salary increases to the politicians every year. Their salary increases should be tied to their performance while in office. If the year ends with a deficit, there should be no salary increase. This would create better accountability for the jobs performed by our politicians.

Some in the news media have publicized the gross inequities in the retirement pay given to members who retire from Congress. Comparisons are made between their retirement benefits and those of large corporations. Our elected congressmen who have been elected by the citizens and have taken an oath to protect the equality of the citizens pass the laws that control their own retirement benefits and their own raises. They can retire with a few years of service at a retirement salary that is several times larger than most citizens. In addition to the setting of the size of the retirement salaries, they also specify a healthy cost-of-living raise for each year which makes the salary grow every year. Compare these retirement salaries to those paid by the largest corporations in the private sector and it will amaze you. This practice will continue until enough citizens speak out and demand some changes. These demands must then be backed up by going to the polls and voting in every election after careful consideration of what your candidates stand for.

Chapter 7
What God Sees in Civil Rights

There has probably not been any movement during the last century that changed the daily lives of people in every state in the United States more than the civil rights movement. There has probably never been anything that needed correction any more than civil rights. We firmly believe that civil rights must be enforced. However, we have considerable reservations about how civil rights are defined and how it has been accomplished. We believe we have created a monster.

When we are young it seems like one hundred years is a long time. Roughly speaking, we might think of one hundred years as a lifetime. Some men and women live longer than one hundred years. Anyone born before 1960 was born less than one hundred years after slavery was abolished by President Lincoln, an act which freed all slaves in the United States. This, of course, did not automatically solve the problems of slavery. While the abolishment of slavery was good and proper, that act alone did not solve all of the problems that years of slavery had created.

Passing a law cannot, in itself, heal the wounds of slavery and racial inequality. There was no effective plan in place to help heal the wounds left by slavery. These wounds have not yet been healed and will never be completely healed until the races have a mutual respect one for another. There was apparently no plan that included respect one for another.

We believe that every citizen, regardless of race, creed, or color should have an equal opportunity. We also believe an equal opportunity is guaranteed by the Constitution. We believe any person who violates the law of the land by denying such opportunity should be prosecuted as stipulated by the law.

We believe we will never have harmony between the races until we have mutual respect one for the other. We have tried to achieve harmony by legislating changes that took away from some in order to give the same to others. Most of the blacks who originally migrated to this country were brought across the ocean on slave ships and sold in this country of ours. Slavery was a terrible part of our history. The way many of the slaves were treated was shameful and sinful. When slavery was abolished by Abraham Lincoln, it was long overdue. Many of our citizens have ancestors who were slaves, and we sympathize with them when we reflect on how their ancestors were mistreated. That is part of our history, and history cannot be changed. What we must do now is deal with the effects of the miscarriage of justice.

There is no person still alive that had any part in creating that part of history. We just believe the civil rights movement of the twentieth century has driven a wedge between the races that will take several generations to heal. The way we approached equal rights was to pass laws that, in effect, took from some citizens and gave to others in an effort to achieve equality. We took pupils out of schools in their neighborhood and bused them to other schools across town in an effort to have a proportionate number of each race in each school. This required buying more buses with money that could have been used to upgrade the classrooms. It also required moving teachers from one school to another to insure a proportionate number of teachers from each race. We believe the required integration of the schools could have been achieved by allowing voluntary movement of pupils and teachers. This would have taken more planning in order to preserve the scholastic standards in all of the schools involved. This in no way refers to either race as being scholastically superior to the other. There are members of all races that are poor students. Some teachers are better teachers than others, and it is not because of race. It is just a fact of life. Everyone is different. In some cases, we have lowered the standards in our schools to insure that an acceptable number of students pass.

We should always try to achieve excellence. Many of us will never reach that goal, but many will. When we mix students by mandate in order to achieve a quota the result is never as good as it was before it was mixed.

Please understand that none of these comments are aimed at either race excluding the other race. There are good black students and there are good white students. Good black students will be good students regardless of which school they attend, and good white students will be good students regardless of which school they attend. The problem arises when standards are relaxed in order to have more students graduate. This practice dilutes the abilities of the graduates who will eventually make up the workforce.

Affirmative action was mandated by Congress during the civil rights movement. This action has violated the Constitutional rights of more citizens than any other law passed by our Congress. Before affirmative action, a business desiring to hire an employee to fill a vacancy in the workforce of the company would interview the applicants for the job. The best qualified applicant, in the opinion of the company, would be hired to fill the vacancy. Affirmative action set quotas that the company was mandated to honor. If the quota of minorities had not been met, then the company was required by law to hire a minority regardless of the qualifications of the other applicants. It is clear that this is a violation of the Constitution. It is also clear that hiring the least qualified applicant can cause a decline in quantity and quality of work. This puts the company in a bad predicament. When the owner of a company invests their money building the company up and making it profitable, he or she should be able to hire applicants based on their qualifications and their worth to the company in order to protect their investment.

Many of us were born into families that were not wealthy. Many of us grew up in families that were downright poor. We were taught to prepare ourselves for the time when we would have the responsibility of supporting our own family. After we assumed the responsibility of supporting a family, we suddenly realized that we were not hired because the hiring company had to fill their quota from another group. For a period of time during the 1970s and 1980s, it seemed that the most discriminated-against group was the white male who was fifty years old and Christian.

Civil rights needed to be dealt with. However, Congress should have given more thought and consideration to the method of achieving equal opportunity so the rights of other citizens would not be violated. It took several years and several generations of slavery and civil rights violation to create the situation we were in at the beginning of the civil rights movement. It is reasonable to assume that the unjust situation cannot be corrected in just a few years. Adequate laws could have been enforced that would guarantee civil rights while, at the same time, resulting in more respect between the races without diluting the qualifications of the workforce.

One only has to consider the hiring practices of the large government agencies to see how affirmative action has destroyed the quality of the workforce. When hiring decisions are based on quotas, it takes more employees to do the job, and the quality of the work is lower than it would be if hiring was based on the qualifications of the job applicants. This results in lower production output, lower quality, and more expense for the taxpayer to cover.

Some members of the black race believe they should receive a large monetary settlement to pay for the sins committed against them by slave owners centuries ago. Those responsible for slavery are long gone. There is now a different generation that had nothing to do with slavery. The fact is the current generation passed laws that guaranteed equality of all races. It is the responsibility of each individual of every race to prepare themselves to support their own families and contribute to the upkeep of this great country of ours. Each citizen must earn their own support by being a contributing member of society. There will always be times when someone needs a helping hand to get them through a bad time. It is right for our government to have programs to help those who need a helping hand, but it is imperative that controls and balances be built into such programs. Without adequate controls, such programs become like a cancer that keeps getting worse and worse. If you can get handouts without working for them there is not much incentive to go to work and earn your living.

Some blacks in the United States have pushed movements to get flags and other signs changed on the grounds that they are offensive because they remind them of slavery. They have tried to get every flag that displays the rebel flag changed. If they would study their history they would know that the Civil War was fought for more than slavery. The rebel flag is a part of the heritage of the Confederacy. While many would do away with these parts of our heritage, they push to preserve symbols of slavery that exist in all black colleges and other institutions. While the white colleges have been forced by law to integrate their institutions, there are still colleges that have essentially all-black student bodies. There is even a United Negro College Fund to help support these black colleges. How can we have it both ways and still achieve mutual respect between the races?

Chapter 8
What God Sees in Riches

God created man in His own image. He gave man the freedom of choice. However, freedom of choice includes the consequences that come with each choice we make. We sometimes forget about the consequences that come with the choices we make. Satan loves to tempt us when we consider financial goals. This is apparently one of the easiest areas in our lives for Satan to win a great victory with his temptations.

Our society seems to revolve around money and how much monetary wealth we can achieve. God speaks very clearly on the subject of monetary wealth. When Jesus was teaching His disciples, a rich man came to him and asked Jesus what he must do to have eternal life. In the nineteenth chapter of Matthew, Jesus answered the rich man.

Matthew 19:21-24

21 If thou wilt be perfect, go and sell that thou hast, and give to the poor, and thou shalt have treasure in heaven: and come and follow me.

22 But when the young man heard that saying, he went away sorrowful: for he had great possessions.

23 Then said Jesus unto his disciples, Verily I say unto you, That a rich man shall hardly enter into the kingdom of heaven.

24 And again I say unto you, It is easier for a camel to go through the eye of a needle, than for a rich man to enter into the kingdom of God.

God is not telling us that acquiring wealth is sinful. He does tell us that our attitude as it relates to our wealth can be sinful. This rich young man wanted to be saved and inherit eternal life, but he loved his riches too much. God knew that riches meant more to him than commitment to God. The consequences were that he had to go away sorrowful because he loved his riches more that he loved God.

God told his disciples that it is hard for a rich man to enter the kingdom of Heaven. It is important to note that God did not say that it is impossible. He still wants all who will come by faith on God's terms to come and be saved from an eternity in Hell. However, God requires commitment.

In the book of Luke, chapter 12, Jesus spoke a parable to his disciples to teach them the consequences of putting too much value on personal wealth.

Luke 12:16-21

16 And he spake a parable unto them, saying, The ground of a certain rich man brought forth plentifully:

17 And he thought within himself, saying, What shall I do, because I have no room where to bestow my fruit?

18 And he said, This will I do: I will pull down my barns, and build greater; and there will I bestow all my fruits and my goods.

19 And I will say to my soul, Soul, thou hast much goods laid up for many years; take thine ease, eat, drink, and be merry.

20 But God said unto him, Thou fool, this night thy soul shall be required of thee: then whose shall those things be, which thou hast provided?

21 So is he that layeth up treasure for himself, and is not rich toward God.

In this parable, the rich man acquired such a large fortune that his barns were not large enough to hold all of it. The rich man made the decision to tear down his barns and build larger ones to hold all of his wealth. God called him a fool because he put so much value in his riches and he would not live to enjoy the fruits of his labor. The benefits of his hard work would be enjoyed by someone else.

Notice that God did not fault the rich man for being successful and earning a great deal of wealth. Verse 21 tells us the rich man accumulated the treasures for himself, but he was not rich toward God. He worshipped his worldly goods rather than worshipping God. The rich man was controlled by his greed.

In the letter that Paul wrote to Timothy, Paul cautions Timothy about putting too much importance on riches.

I Timothy 6:9-11

9 But they that will be rich fall into temptation and a snare, and into many foolish and hurtful lusts, which drown men in destruction and perdition.

10 For the love of money is the root of all evil: which while some coveted after, they have erred from the faith, and pierced themselves through with many sorrows.

11 But thou, O man of God, flee these things; and follow after righteousness, godliness, faith, love, patience, meekness.

If we love riches more than we love God, we make ourselves more receptive to the temptations of Satan. Our love for riches makes us love Satan more than we love God. Without God's help we cannot compete with Satan and his temptations. From the root of evil grows temptations by Satan that are making a mockery of the Christian foundation upon which this country was founded. We must continually be in a spirit of prayer and ask God to give us the strength to stand against the temptations of Satan.

The love of money causes some to stray from the will of God. The love for money fills our heart with greed which will control our relationship with God as well as our relationship with our fellow men if we allow it. Greed grows into lust for things that are desirable to us but which we do not possess. Our society is filled with illicit sexual activity that is driven by this lust.

There was a time when our courts and our governments were controlled by godly principles. Greed and lust for power have eroded the fabric of our courts and our government. Many of our officers of the court and our government leaders are more interested in earthly success and riches than they are in seeking and doing the will of God. This is plunging our society into the pits of Hell. How long will God allow us to make such a mockery of His creation?

The love of money not only leads to greed, but it also leads to impatience. We want to have everything right now. God expects us to earn our living by the sweat of our brow. We expect riches to come immediately. We want to live too fast. This is evident when we look at what we see on television. It is evident in the godless lives that are evident in the movie industry. It is evident in the workplace.

Greed has also grown out of control in our churches. Individual churches of all denominations seem to be in a contest to see who can build the largest, most luxurious church building. We sometimes forget the mission of the local church which is to teach the lost as Jesus taught his disciples. We forget that a church building is a meeting place for the church body which is made up of those who have accepted Jesus Christ as their Savior and asked him to forgive them of their sins. We sometimes take too much pride in the worldly riches than we do in helping lost people come to a saving knowledge of Jesus Christ. We neglect the teaching of the Bible but organize worldly activities that will attract more young people to our church. While it is true that we should attract young people to our church, it is also true that they need to understand what the church is. We must have programs to teach our young and old more about what it means to be a Christian. This is especially important today with the efforts made to remove all evidence of God from our schools. God does not judge the church by how many members the church has or how many trips the church has organized. God judges the church by how many lost souls the church has brought into the fold.

God expects us to be good stewards of the abilities and opportunities which He gives us. He expects us to prosper as long as we remember to put God first and never place more importance on prosperity than on God. In the book of Matthew Jesus teaches the disciples about stewardship with the following parable.

Matthew 25:14-30

14 For the kingdom of heaven is as a man traveling into a far country, who called his own servants, and delivered unto them his goods.

15 And unto one he gave five talents, to another two, and to another one; to every man according to his several ability; and straightway took his journey.

16 Then he that received the five talents went and traded with the same, and made them other five talents.

17 And likewise he that had received two, he also gained other two.

18 But he that had received one went and digged in the earth, and hid his lord's money.

19 After a long time the lord of those servants cometh, and reckoneth with them.

20 And so he that had received five talents came and brought other five talents, saying, Lord, thou deliverest unto me five talents: behold I have gained beside them five talents more.

21 His lord said unto him, Well-done, thou good and faithful servant: thou hast been faithful over a few things, I will make thee ruler over many things: enter thou into the joy of thy lord.

22 He also that had received two talents came and said, Lord, thou deliverest unto me two talents; behold, I have gained two other talents beside them.

23 His lord said unto him, Well-done good and faithful servant; thou hast been faithful over a few things, I will make thee ruler over many things: enter thou into the joy of thy lord.

24 Then he which had received the one talent came and said, Lord, I knew thee that thou art an hard man, reaping where thou hast not sown, and gathering where thou hast not strewed:

25 And I was afraid, and went and hid thy talent in the earth: lo, there thou hast that is thine.

26 His lord answered and said unto him, Thou wicked and slothful servant, thou knewest that I reap where I sowed not, and gather where I have not strewed:

27 Thou oughtest therefore to have put my money to the exchangers, and then at my coming I should have received mine own with usury.

28 Take therefore the talent from him, and give it unto him which hath ten talents

29 For unto every one that hath shall be given, and he shall have abundance: but from him that hath not shall be taken away even that which he hath.

30 And cast ye the unprofitable servant into outer darkness; there shall be weeping and gnashing of teeth.

In this parable, a rich man was going on a trip. He called three of his servants together and gave them instructions to be followed while he was away. To one he gave five talents, to another he gave two talents, and to another he gave one talent. A talent represented a form of money. He gave each servant different amounts depending on their abilities.

When the rich man returned from his trip he called the servants together for an accounting of what they had done with what he had entrusted them. The first servant had been entrusted with five talents. He had used them wisely and they had multiplied and become ten talents. The second servant had been entrusted with two talents. He had also used them wisely and the two talents had multiplied and become four talents. The third servant had been entrusted with one talent. He was afraid that he would lose the talent and anger his master, so he buried the talent so it would not be lost.

The master rewarded the servant who had received five talents and the servant who had received two talents. The servant who had been given one talent was rebuked by the master after which the master took the one talent and gave it to the servant who had made five talents grow into ten talents.

We are all like these three servants. God has given each of us certain abilities which God expects us to use wisely. If we will use these abilities wisely we will prosper according to our abilities. God expects us to prosper according to our abilities. Prosperity only becomes a sin when our greed makes us love our wealth more than we love God.

Chapter 9
How God Sees Homosexuality

Homosexuality has become more acceptable by society to the point that it endangers the family unit. God's people must seek God's help in dealing with this problem. What does God see when he looks at our attitude about homosexuality?

In the book of Leviticus, chapter 18, God commands Moses concerning how the children of Israel are to interact with one another. In order to understand God's message to his children, one should read the entire chapter. We will address some key verses, but highly recommend that the entire chapter be read.

Leviticus 18:1-5

1 And the Lord spake unto Moses, saying,

2 Speak unto the children of Israel, and say unto them, I am the Lord your God.

3 After the doings of the land of Egypt, wherein ye dwelt, shall ye not do: and after the doings of the land of Canaan, whither I bring you, shall ye not do: neither shall ye walk in their ordinances.

4 Ye shall do my judgements, and keep mine ordinances, to walk therein: I am the Lord your God.

5 Ye shall therefore keep my statutes, and my judgements: which if a man do, he shall live in them: I am the Lord.

God used Moses to lead God's people out of the land of Egypt to the land of Canaan. God gave Moses certain rules which they were to follow. Verses 6 through 21 give a detailed definition of who is near of kin and instructs His people concerning acts that are not allowed with near of kin. These acts were practiced by some of the people in Egypt and in Canaan. God commanded his people to not perform such acts.

Leviticus 18:22-30 gives us God's statutes concerning homosexuality.

Leviticus 18:22-30

22 Thou shalt not lie with mankind, as with womankind: it is abomination.

23 Neither shalt thou lie with any beast to defile thyself therewith: neither shall any woman stand before a beast to lie down thereto: it is confusion.

24 Defile not ye yourselves in any of these things: for in all these the nations are defiled which I cast out before you:

25 And the land is defiled: therefore I do visit the iniquity thereof upon it, and the land itself vomiteth out her inhabitants.

26 Ye shall therefore keep my statutes and my judgements, and shall not commit any of these abominations; neither any of your own nation, nor any stranger that sojourneth among you:

27 (For all these abominations have the men of the land done, which were before you, and the land is defiled;)

28 That the land spew not you out also, when ye defile it, as it spewed out the nations that were before you.

29 For whosoever shall commit any of these abominations, even the souls that commit them shall be cut off from among their people.

30 Therefore shall ye keep mine ordinance, that ye commit not any one of these abominable customs, which were committed before you, and that you defile not yourselves therein: I am the Lord your God.

In verse 22 God tells us it is an abomination for a man to lie with another man as he would with a woman.

God tells us in verse 23 that neither a man nor a woman shall lie down with an animal.

Verse 24 commands us to not defile ourselves by participating in any of these unnatural acts which were practices by the people who inhabited the lands from which God had driven them so the lands could be settled by God's children led out of Egypt by Moses.

In verses 25-29 God speaks to us about the previous inhabitants of the Promised Land and their sins and how God judged them and punished them for their sinful living. God warns His people that they must obey His commands and refrain from such sinful practices. The failure of God's people to do so will result in them being driven from the land like the previous inhabitants were driven out.

God emphasizes His command to his people that they refrain from committing these abominable customs and reminds them that He is the Lord their God.

We sometimes wonder how God who loves us so much can

bring His wrath down upon us when we refuse to follow God's commands. We could take lessons from God when we are faced with discipline problems with our children. Some have called it tough love. God shows us some tough love when we continue to practice unrighteousness. In the first chapter of Romans, God speaks to us again about the wrath of God.

Romans 1:16-19

16 For I am not ashamed of the gospel of Christ: for it is the power of God unto salvation to every one that believeth; to the Jew first, and also to the Greek.

17 For therein is the righteousness of God revealed from faith to faith: as it is written, The just shall live by faith.

18 For the wrath of God is revealed from heaven against all ungodliness and unrighteousness of men, who hold the truth in unrighteousness;

19 Because that which may be known of God is manifest in them; for God hath showed it unto them.

The apostle Paul is speaking to all of God's people in Rome. Paul reaffirms the fact that he is not ashamed of the gospel of Christ for it is the power of God unto salvation for everyone who believes, including the Jews and the Gentiles. Paul tells us that the wrath of God is revealed from Heaven against all ungodliness and unrighteousness.

Turning our attention back to the book of Exodus we find a warning from God in the twentieth chapter of Exodus.

Exodus 20:1-6

1 And God spake all these words, saying,

2 I am the Lord thy God, which have brought thee out of the land of Egypt, out of the house of bondage.

3 Thou shalt have no other gods before me.

4 Thou shalt not make unto thee any graven image, or any likeness of any thing that is in heaven above, or that is in the earth beneath, or that is in the water under the earth:

5 Thou shalt not bow down thyself to them, nor serve them: for I the Lord thy God am a jealous God, visiting the iniquity of the fathers upon the children unto the third and fourth generation of them that hate me;

6 And showing mercy unto thousands of them that love me, and keep my commandments.

God spoke these words to Moses after Moses had led God's people out of bondage. The people were glad to be rescued from the bondage in Egypt and had begun to celebrate a little too much to the extent that they sometimes forgot about the goodness and mercy of God. They began to worship various idols which they allowed to take the place of God in their lives.

God reminded His people who it was that had rescued them from bondage. God reminded His people that the sins which they were committing would not only alienate them from God, but would also affect the way their generations of children would be affected.

In the first chapter of Genesis God tells us what He created. The second chapter of Genesis gives us more information about how the creation took place.

Genesis 1:26-27

26 And God said, Let us make man in our image, after our likeness: and let them have dominion over the fish of the sea, and over the fowl of the air, and over the cattle, and over all the earth, and over every creeping thing that creepeth upon the earth.

27 So God created man in his own image, in the image of God created he him; male and female created he them.

God created man in His own image which indicates that man was without sin when he was created. Man was given dominion over all that God had created to care for God's creations. God created male and female. God did not give man and woman the option of personal sexual preference which is a term our society has added.

Genesis 2:18-24

18 And the Lord God said, It is not good that the man should be alone; I will make him a help meet for him.

19 And out of the ground the Lord God formed every beast of the field, and every fowl of the air; and brought them unto Adam to see what he would call them: and whatsoever Adam called every living creature, that was the name thereof.

20 And Adam gave names to all cattle, and to the fowl of the air, and to every beast of the field; but for Adam there was not found a help meet for him.

21 And the Lord God caused a deep sleep to fall upon Adam, and he slept: and he took one of his ribs, and closed up the flesh instead thereof;

22 And the rib, which the Lord God had taken from man, made he a woman, and brought her unto the man.

23 And Adam said, This is now bone of my bones, and flesh of my flesh: she shall be called Woman, because she was taken out of Man.

24 Therefore shall a man leave his father and his mother, and shall cleave unto his wife: and they shall be one flesh.

In order to make man complete God created a woman to be a help meet or partner. Adam called this partner woman because God had made her from a rib he had taken from man. God then tells us a man shall leave his father and mother and shall cleave unto his wife and they shall be one. This is God's plan for a proper marriage.

God created man in His own image. Man was created perfect which tells us that man was without sin. God gave man a free will or the ability to make choices. Along with the ability to make choices God also gave man the consequences that come as a result of the choices which man makes. After Adam and Eve sinned man was no longer without sin.

God commanded man to serve no other God, and the sins of the fathers will be passed on to the third and fourth generation of them that hate God. "Those that hate God" refers to those who do not obey God's commandments. God tells us that He shows mercy unto them that love Him and keep His commandments. Man chooses to serve God, or not to serve God. Man must live with the consequences of his choices.

Since God created man in His image it is inconceivable that God created some that were half man and half woman, or man with the mind and characteristics of a woman. While it is possible that a man might be born with such characteristics, if one believes the Bible he must assume that these characteristics were not created by God but were the result of sins that were passed down through generations as a result of the sins of the fathers. These characteristics can be overcome by faith and allegiance to God.

It is also true that some men are born with a physical characteristic that is womanly. Some women are born with a physical characteristic that is manly. These unusual traits are no different from other birth defects. It is difficult to understand how these birth defects occur. Some birth defects can be corrected by the medical profession. It is difficult to understand what causes these defects.

The problem that we are addressing is the growing number of healthy individuals who make a conscious decision that they are not happy with their gender and choose to live as a member of the opposite sex. This homosexual activity is an abomination to God according to his teachings in the Bible. This problem is growing to monumental proportions to the extent that our political leaders are making laws that permit homosexual couples to marry and even adopt children. This is an abomination to God and we must wonder how long God will permit such mockery of God's creation.

God created the heavens and the earth. God created man to care for that which He had created, and He made woman from a rib which He took from Adam. God created man and woman according to His specific plan. He gave man the responsibility of having dominion over all of that which He had created. It would be difficult, if not impossible, to separate all of the responsibilities of man from those of woman. God's plan calls for man and woman to function as one body in the form of husband and wife with each having very specific responsibilities in order to have a perfect union. When the husband falls short in some of his responsibilities, the wife, in some cases, can shoulder some of the responsibilities where the husband fell short. The same is true when the wife falls short and the husband shoulders some of the wife's responsibilities. There are, however, some of the husband's responsibilities that the wife is not physically or mentally able to shoulder. There are also some of the wife's responsibilities that the husband is not able to shoulder. These situations are responsible for creating a family unit that is not perfect. It creates family problems that can be dealt with when we let God lead us. This, by no means, makes the husband less than a man nor the wife less than a woman.

We are experiencing a sexual revolution such as we have not seen in recent history. This revolution is fueled by the media on television and the movies. There is too much emphasis placed on our distorted definition of equality. Man and woman were created by God with entirely different purposes, different needs, and different characteristics. Man cannot adequately become a woman, and woman cannot adequately become a man. Any attempt to do so will be playing games with God's plan and cannot be looked on favorably by God.

A child begins to learn the moment he or she is born and never quits learning until life is over. The younger a child is, the more the child learns because he or she is eager to learn until the eagerness is slowed down by well-meaning parents. As simple an act as dressing a boy like a girl, or a girl like a boy, can alter what the child is learning. Parents often think it is cute to see their child imitate the opposite sex. The child absorbs the parent's action as their approval and it becomes part of their learning. Boys learn to be men by playing with boy toys, and girls learn to be ladies by playing with girl toys.

No one action by the parents will properly teach children the incorrect values, but all of their actions together can certainly give them the wrong signal.

Chapter 10
How God Sees Heaven and Hell

What is Heaven like, and what is Hell like? The Bible tells us much about Heaven and Hell. When we think about Heaven and Hell the way God describes them in the Bible, it is hard to comprehend what they are like. Some individuals believe they know exactly where Heaven is and where Hell is. No one on earth knows where they are. The location is not important. The important thing to understand is that Heaven is where God lives and Hell is where Satan lives.

The key to understanding the Bible is making sure we have a personal relationship with God through faith. We must understand that the Bible is God speaking to us. We must accept God's Word by faith. The more we study the Bible, the stronger our faith becomes, and the more God reveals to us. Those who are born-again Christians are committed to God and to God's Word which is the Bible.

Let us look at some of the references that talk about Heaven. In Exodus 20, God is telling Moses what he is to say to the children of Israel.

Exodus 20:22-23

22 And the Lord said unto Moses, Thus thou shalt say unto the children of Israel, Ye have seen that I talked with you from heaven.

23 Ye shall not make with me gods of silver, neither shall ye make unto you gods of gold.

God told Moses that He had talked with him from Heaven. God lives in Heaven.

In Deuteronomy 33, God spoke to Moses about the many precious things that they had received from Heaven.

Deuteronomy 33:13-16

13 And of Joseph he said, Blessed of the Lord be his land, for the precious things of heaven, for the dew, and for the deep that coucheth beneath,

14 And for the precious fruits brought forth by the sun, and for the precious things put forth by the moon,

15 And for the chief things of the ancient mountains, and for the precious things of the lasting hills,

16 And for the precious things of the earth and the fullness thereof, and for the good will of him that dwelt in the bush: let the blessing come upon the head of Joseph, and upon the top of the head of him that was separated from his brethren.

The precious things supplied by God from Heaven included the dew and precious fruits brought forth by the sun and the moon. God also supplied precious things in the mountains and hills. All of these things were supplied by God from Heaven.

In Ecclesiastes 5, God reminds his people again that God is in Heaven.

Ecclesiastes 5:2

Be not rash with thy mouth, and let not thine heart be hasty to utter anything before God: For God is in heaven, and thou upon the earth: therefore let thy words be few.

In Jeremiah 23, God reminds his people that he is omnipresent.

Jeremiah 23:24

24 Can any hide himself in secret places that I shall not see him? saith the Lord. Do not I fill Heaven and earth? saith the Lord.

Nobody can hide where God cannot see him. God is everywhere in Heaven and in the earth.

In Matthew 5, God tells us that our reward is in Heaven.

Matthew 5:11-12

11 Blessed are ye, when men shall revile you, and persecute you, and shall say all manner of evil against you falsely, for my sake.

12 Rejoice, and be exceeding glad; for great is your reward in heaven; for so persecuted they the prophets which were before you.

God blesses His people when we are reviled and persecuted and talked about falsely for God's sake. God tells us that we should rejoice and be glad because our reward in Heaven will be great. God reminds us that we are not the first ones to be persecuted for God's sake because prophets were persecuted before us.

In Matthew 6, Jesus taught his disciples to pray.

Matthew 6:9-10

9 After this manner therefore pray ye: Our Father which art in heaven, Hallowed be thy name.

10 Thy kingdom come. Thy will be done in earth, as it is in heaven.

Jesus told his disciples to address their prayers to God who is in Heaven. God went on to teach His disciples to ask God for His will to be done in earth like it is in Heaven. These verses in the Bible are a part of what has been referred to as the model prayer.

In Luke 10, it is recorded that Jesus sent out a group of seventy believers in teams of two each, into cities where Jesus Himself would visit, to prepare the way for His visit. God had empowered them with special gifts, or powers, for this purpose.

Luke 10:17-20

17 And the seventy returned again with joy, saying, Lord, even the devils are subject to us through thy name.

18 And he said unto them, I beheld Satan as lightening fall from heaven.

19 Behold, I give unto you power to tread on serpents and scorpions, and over all the power of the enemy; and nothing shall by any means hurt you.

20 Notwithstanding, in this rejoice not, that the spirits are subject unto you; but rather rejoice, because your names are written in heaven.

The seventy returned and reported to Jesus with joy the things they had experienced with the special powers which they had been given. Jesus told them not to rejoice because they were able to accomplish these things, but rejoice because their names were written in Heaven.

In John 3, Jesus speaks again about Heaven.

John 3:13

13 And no man has ascended up to heaven, but he that came down from heaven, even the Son of man which is in heaven.

Jesus tells His followers that no man has ever ascended up to Heaven but one who had come down from Heaven. When Jesus ascended up to Heaven after He had been buried in the tomb, Jesus ascended up to Heaven in His bodily form. When the saved on earth die and go to Heaven, they will not go in their bodily form. They will go to Heaven with new bodies.

In Philippians 3, Paul writes to the churches at Philippi.

Philippians 3:20

20 For our conversation is in heaven; from whence also we look for the Savior, the Lord Jesus Christ.

Those who are saved should look to Heaven where the Lord Jesus Christ is.

We have referenced several references from the Bible about Heaven, what it is like, and where it is. Now we turn our attention to Hell and where it is and what the nature of Hell is.

In Matthew 10, Jesus was teaching His disciples before sending them out to do his work. He gave them words of encouragement to prepare them for the occasions when they would be persecuted and maybe even killed.

Matthew 10:28

28 And fear not them that kill the body, but are not able to kill the soul: but rather fear him which is able to destroy both body and soul in hell.

Jesus taught the disciples to not fear those who would persecute them. Rather, He encouraged them to fear the one who is able to kill the body and soul in Hell. This is a reference to Satan who tempts God's people from Hell where Satan lives.

In Matthew 16, Jesus is teaching His disciples and asked them who men say that He is. When they told Him that some say that He is John the Baptist, Elijah, Jeremiah, or one of the prophets, Jesus asked His disciples who they say He is. Simon Peter answered Him by saying that He is Christ the Son of the living God. Matthew 16:18 records the words that Jesus spoke to them in response to Peter's answer.

Matthew 16:18

18 And I say unto thee, That thou art Peter, and upon this rock I will build my church; and the gates of hell shall not prevail against it.

When Jesus said He would build His church upon this rock, the rock referred to the words of Peter that Jesus is Christ the son of the living God. Some will say that God built the church upon Peter, but that is a misinterpretation of the point that God was making to His disciples. Jesus came to establish the church which was built upon Jesus Christ, the Son of man.

In Luke 16, Jesus spoke to the Pharisees who criticized and mocked Him concerning their riches and covetous attitude. The Pharisees held themselves in very high esteem and they believed their worth was above everyone else.

Luke 16:19-26

19 There was a certain rich man, which was clothed in purple and fine linen, and fared sumptuously every day:

20 And there was a certain beggar named Lazarus, which was laid at his gate, full of sores,

21 And desiring to be fed with the crumbs which fell from the rich man's table: moreover the dogs came and licked his sores.

22 And it came to pass, that the beggar died, and was carried by the angels into Abraham's bosom: the rich man also died, and was buried;

23 And in hell he lifted up his eyes, being in torments, and seeth Abraham afar off, and Lazarus in his bosom.

24 And he cried and said, Father Abraham, have mercy on me, and send Lazarus, that he may dip the tip of his finger in water, and cool my tongue; for I am tormented in this flame.

25 But Abraham said, Son, remember that thou in thy lifetime receivest the good things, and likewise Lazarus evil things: but now he is comforted, and thou are tormented.

26 And besides all this, between us and you there is a great gulf fixed: so that they that would pass from hence to you cannot; neither can they pass to us, that would come from thence.

Jesus told the Pharisees the story of the rich man and Lazarus. The rich man had plenty to eat every day. Lazarus was a poor beggar who would beg for the crumbs that fell from the rich man's table to the floor.

The rich man died and was buried. Lazarus died and went to Heaven. The rich man lifted up his eyes in Hell and in torment. He cried out to Father Abraham and begged him to send Lazarus to dip the tip of his finger in water and cool the tongue of the rich man because the rich man was tormented in the flames of Hell.

Father Abraham reminded the rich man that he received good things during his lifetime and Lazarus received evil things but is now comforted while the rich man is tormented. He went on to explain to the rich man that there is a great gulf fixed between Heaven and Hell so none can pass from one to the other.

We have noted numerous references from the Bible about Heaven and Hell that should give us an understanding about the nature and purpose of Heaven and Hell. Many of the teachings of Jesus were done using symbolic descriptions. No one has ever seen Heaven or Hell. Whether the descriptions of Heaven and Hell were symbolic or literal descriptions should not matter to us. If we were to assume that the descriptions are symbolic, there is enough evidence in the Bible to convince us that Heaven is a glorious place beyond our imagination. It is described as streets of gold and a place where there is no sickness, no wars, and no enmity. Hell is described as a place with everlasting fire and a place where nobody can help to ease the soul that is there.

In Matthew 7, Jesus is teaching the multitudes.

Matthew 7:13-14

13 Enter ye in at the strait gate: for wide is the gate, and broad is the way, that leadeth to destruction, and many there be which go in thereat:

14 Because strait is the gate, and narrow is the way, which leadeth unto life, and few there be that find it.

In these verses Jesus told the multitudes that the path to destruction is a wide path and many will choose this path. The final destination is everlasting torment in Hell.

Jesus then told the multitudes that the path to life is a narrow path and few will choose this path. The final destination is everlasting life in Heaven.

We have referenced numerous references in the Bible about Heaven and Hell. We highly recommend that you study these references and read the chapters in which they are found in the Bible.

Based upon what we have learned from these references, we must conclude that Heaven is where God lives and Hell is where Satan lives. God has prepared a place in Heaven for the saved on earth. God also prepared a place in Hell for those on earth that are not saved. Heaven is a place that is so glorious that it is beyond description. Hell is a place of eternal torment beyond our imagination.

There are two roads from which we must choose the road we will follow. One road is narrow and leads to everlasting life in Heaven. Those who choose this road must accept Jesus Christ, the Son of God, as their personal Savior. This choice requires faith in God and commitment to ask God to forgive us for our sins. The other road is wide and easy to travel. This road is easy to follow. There is no commitment and no faith required for traveling down this road.

What is not understood by many is the fact that each individual will travel one of these roads. This is part of God's plan to reward those who commit themselves to Him. We cannot decide that we will not participate in this plan. To do so will be a decision to travel the wide road to everlasting torment in Hell.

God is giving us a choice. It is up to each of us which road we will choose.